TECHNOLOGY:
BLUEPRINTS OF THE FUTURE

TECHNOLOGY:
BLUEPRINTS OF THE FUTURE

The
Internet
Inside and Out

by
Michael Eck

Illustrations
Leonello Calvetti

The Rosen Publishing Group's

New York

Published in 2002 in North America
by The Rosen Publishing Group, Inc., New York

First Edition

Book Design:
Andrea Dué s.r.l.
Florence, Italy

Illustrations:
Leonello Calvetti
and
Alessandro Baldanzi, Alessandro Bartolozzi

Editor:
Joanne Randolph

Photo Research: Jason Moring

Library of Congress Cataloging-in-Publication Data

Eck, Michael.
The Internet : inside and out / by Michael Eck. — 1st ed.
p. cm. — (Technology—blueprints of the future)
Includes bibliographical references and index.
ISBN 0-8239-6108-7 (library binding)
1. Internet—Juvenile literature. [1. Internet.] I. Title. II. Series.
TK5105.875.I57 E245 2002
004.67'8—dc2
2001000139
Manufactured in Italy by Eurolitho S.p.A., Milan

Contents

The Internet and You

One of the most interesting and exciting aspects of the Internet is its openness. In theory anyone can offer information, and anyone can have access to it. However there are still some barriers regarding access that must be overcome, including availability, cost, and ease of use for people with disabilities.

The technology of the Internet is equally open. All of its technical standards are available for free. Anyone can build a new application and place it on the Internet. In fact a lot of the new ideas for Internet applications come from users who think of new ways to use the network and then try them out. The World Wide Web was developed by Tim Berners-Lee, a user of the Internet!

What does that mean to you? For one thing, it means that you may be the next person to invent a new Internet application that captures everyone's attention. If you have a problem, and the Internet helps you solve it, maybe it will help solve that problem for other people as well. That is how the world of technology progresses: People discover problems and solutions for themselves, and they share those solutions with others. Sometimes the solutions are free, and sometimes they turn into businesses!

I am confident that some of you will invent some very interesting solutions to problems you encounter, making the Internet even more useful than it is today. When you do, I look forward to learning about it.

Meanwhile I hope you'll find this book fun and thought provoking.

Warmest wishes,

Vint Cerf

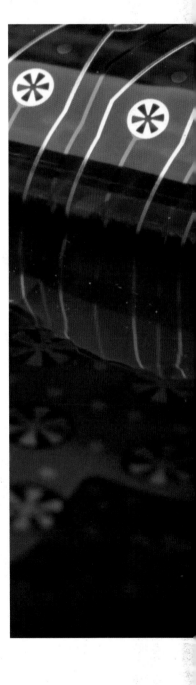

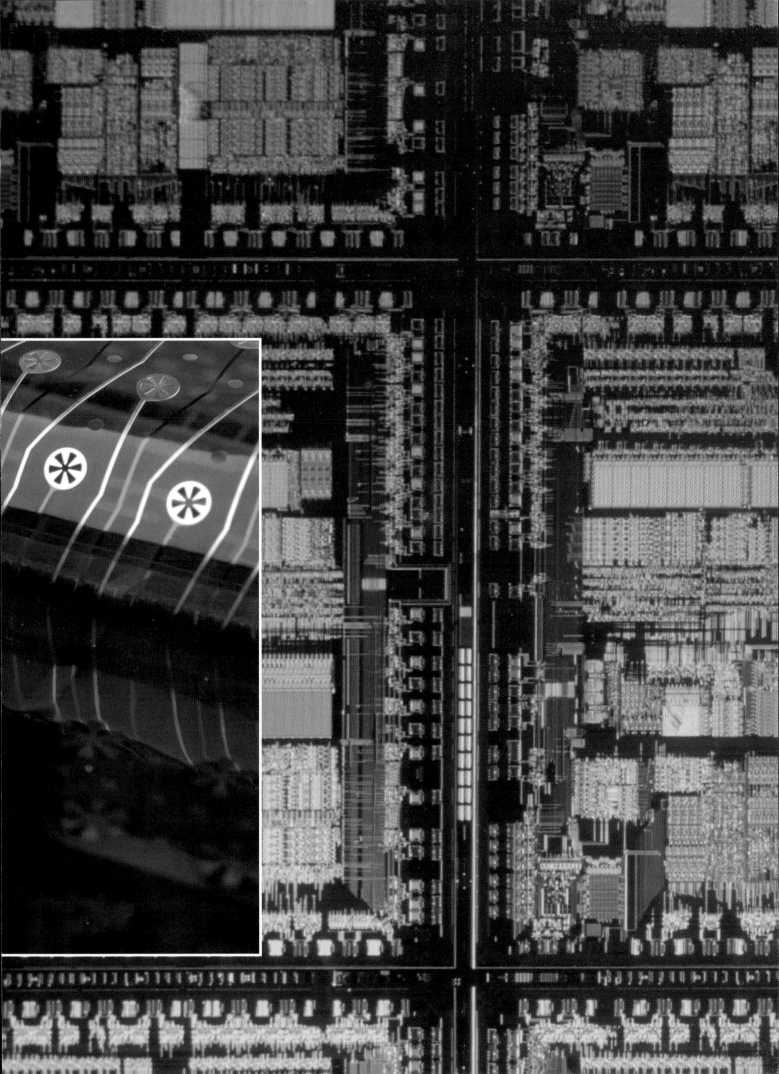

What is the Internet, Anyway?

The Internet is difficult to define. It is a giant collection of interconnected computer networks that spans the world using fiber-optic cables, radio towers, and satellites. It also includes vast resources of information and programs that reside on computers connected to the Internet. Any Internet connection in the world can access huge amounts of data from the U.S. Library of Congress in Washington, D.C., the British Museum in London, England, the Louvre in Paris, France, and many other places around the world. The Internet also includes music, video, and 3-D graphics. People can use the Internet to pay bills, buy dog food, play interactive computer games, or make telephone calls. The uses of the Internet are only limited by human imagination.

The Internet is dynamic. The uses of the Internet change daily, and the world's Internet infrastructure grows and changes constantly. Cables and specialized computers connect millions of computers around the world. These interconnected systems send trillions of pieces of data around the world every day. The services and information available on the Internet's computers are also part of the Internet itself. Together they function as a global information system used by people around the world.

The Internet functions across international boundaries, in every language, and on every type of computer. The designers of the first networks that would grow into the Internet used standard rules so the operation of the Internet would be easy for users. Because the rules that computers use to communicate on the Internet are universal, any computer can communicate with any other. This standardization continued with the development of the World Wide Web.

As you will see, the Internet is a complicated mosaic of computers and software working together to provide information and services to the entire world. It is a dynamic, growing system that constantly changes. The Internet has great potential, because it is open to anyone with access to a computer and an Internet connection. We each have the opportunity to contribute to the future of the Internet as it expands to reach every person on Earth.

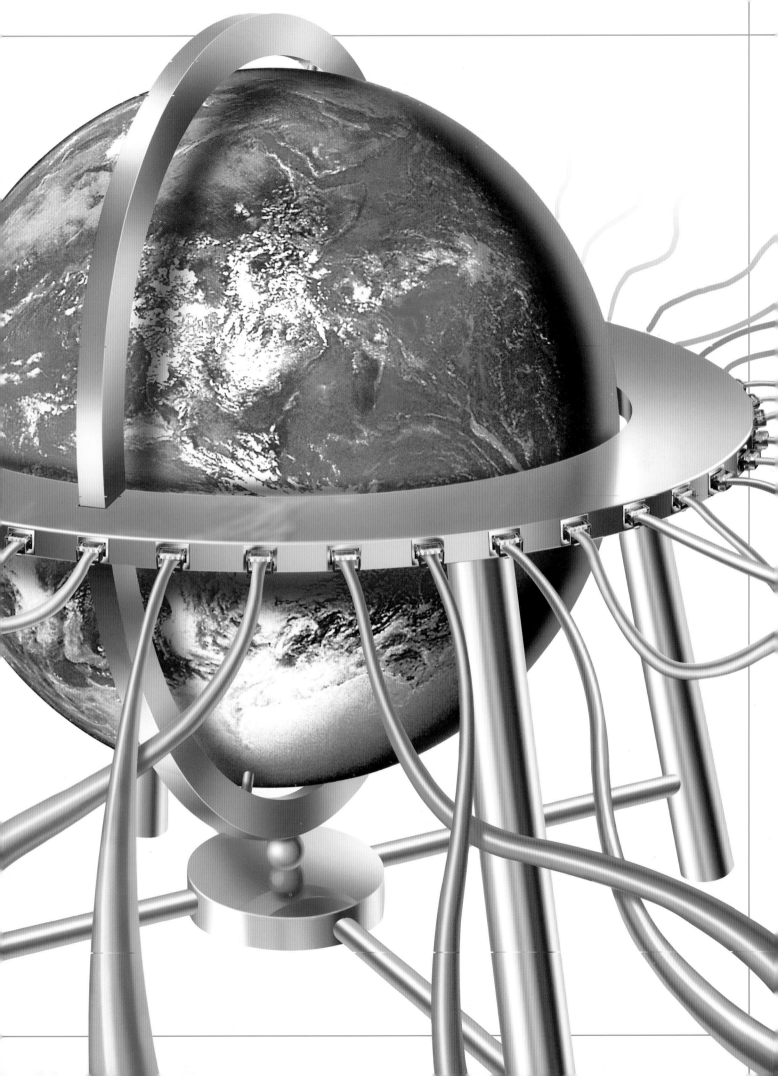

Laying the Foundation

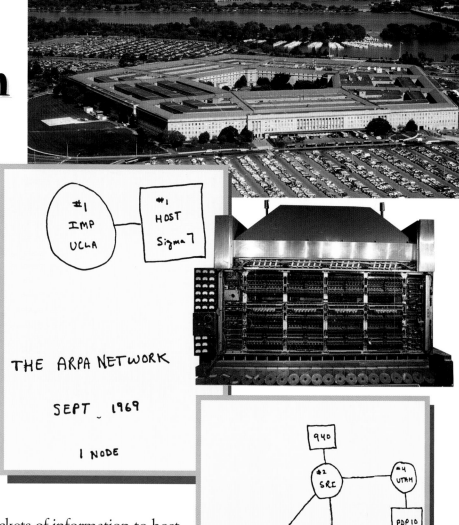

THE ARPA NETWORK

SEPT 1969

1 NODE

THE ARPA NETWORK

DEC 1969

Work toward building the Internet began as a U.S. government project to develop new ways for computers to communicate over long distances. In 1969, the Advanced Research Projects Agency (ARPA) of the U.S. Department of Defense awarded a contract to the small firm of Bolt, Beranek & Newman (BBN) to design and to build an experimental network. Larger companies, like AT&T, had said such a network could not be built! BBN's team, at four universities in California and Utah, connected their computers using new machines called Interface Message Processors (IMPs) and high-speed telephone lines. The IMPs delivered packets of information to host computers. The host computers used the packets for software programs. Dividing the functions, or jobs, between different types of computers and different protocols became a standard in designing networks. This new network, known as the ARPA Network, or ARPANET, was the first long-distance computer network.

ARPANET was based on packet switching. Before the ARPANET, two computers could communicate remotely only through modems that connected them directly to each other. In packet switching, computers no longer needed to be directly connected to communicate with each other. Instead, intermediate computers, now called routers, could look at each packet and determine its destination. The router would either send it directly to the destination, or to another router that was closer. With packet switching, messages were broken into smaller packets of specified lengths. Instead of sending an entire book at once, packet switching would send it one page at a time. Smaller packet sizes allowed many computers to use the same network simultaneously, because they didn't have to wait for the first computer to finish sending its message.

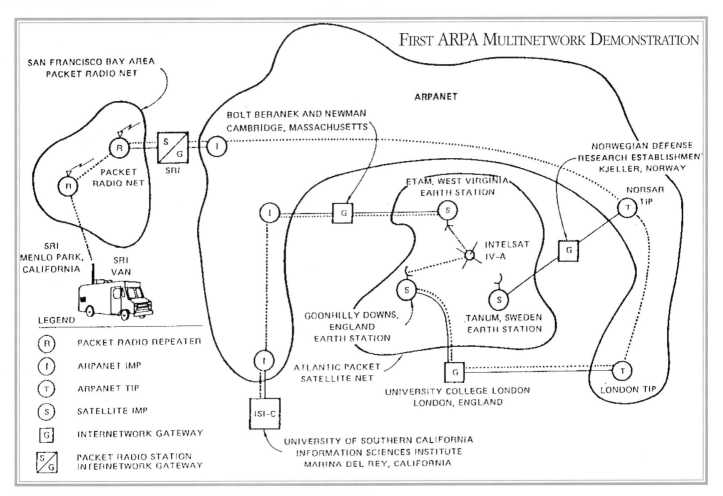

Left, top: The Pentagon Building housed the Advanced Research Projects Agency that was responsible for the birth of the first long-distance computer network.

Left, middle: A 1965 computer

Left, two drawings: These drawings show the earliest stage of the ARPANET. There were, at first, just two nodes. By December 1969, there were four nodes.

Below: The UCLA campus, shown below, was one of the four nodes that made up the ARPANET.

Computer networks grew throughout the 1970s. In 1971, the ARPANET expanded to 15 locations, or nodes, from its original four. ARPANET and other networks communicated through land-based telephone cables, but other networks like the Packet Radio Network (PRNET) used radio. Engineers tested the first mobile network by driving a radio-equipped van around the San Francisco Bay area. However, these different networks had no means of communication with each other, because they used different protocols and formats to send data. The engineers working on ARPANET wanted to connect the growing number of separate networks. Because each network used different hardware and software for networking computers together, Vinton Cerf and Robert Kahn began working on a new system in 1973, to enable diverse networks to connect to each other. This required writing software that could be used on any network. The result of their work was the Transmission Control Protocol (TCP), later separated into TCP and IP. Cerf and Kahn also proposed using gateways to transfer different packets between different types of networks. Gateways would later be called routers. TCP/IP and routers would allow universal protocols, or protocols that could be understood by any computer, and transmission of data across any type of network. These ideas allowed the Internet to grow, because many networks now could connect together.

Protocols and Routers

A computer processes data using binary digits, or bits. A bit is either a 0 or a 1. An active electrical signal is a digital 1, and an inactive signal is a 0. Computers group bits into groups of eight, called bytes. Bits and bytes are the building blocks of information on the Internet. Computers arrange bits and bytes into groups called packets. A packet is a specified number of bits arranged in a particular format. Every e-mail, video clip, or picture is broken down into packets containing bytes of data.

For the Internet to work, computers need to communicate with each other. Computers use special rules, called protocols, to communicate for different purposes. There are many types of protocols, and they are essential for Internet communications. The rules used for protocols specify how to arrange the bits inside each packet, so that each computer knows where to find specific information.

Two of the most important protocols on the Internet are Transmission Control Protocol (TCP) and Internet Protocol (IP). TCP makes sure packets are numbered and put together properly. Sometimes messages are too big to send all at once, so TCP splits the data into smaller packets. It's like numbering all the pages in a book, sending them one page at a time, and putting the book together at the other end. If one of the pages is missing, TCP tells the sending computer which pages are missing and asks for another copy. TCP also checks each packet for errors, and, if there are errors, asks for another copy of the packet. TCP is a reliable protocol, because it has this error-checking process.

IP allows computers to identify themselves through special numbers called IP addresses. An IP address is a set of numbers separated by periods. An example is 172.16.152.5. IP addresses are used to identify computers for delivering packets, just like postal addresses are used to deliver mail. TCP and IP usually work

Below: An e-mail message comes in packets, represented by the packages in carts below. The packets are divided and are given a number that will allow the computer at the destination to put the information back together again in the proper order.

The packets are sent along different paths, or routes. Routes are chosen based on the shortest or most available path that will take the least amount of time possible between the sender's computer and the destination.

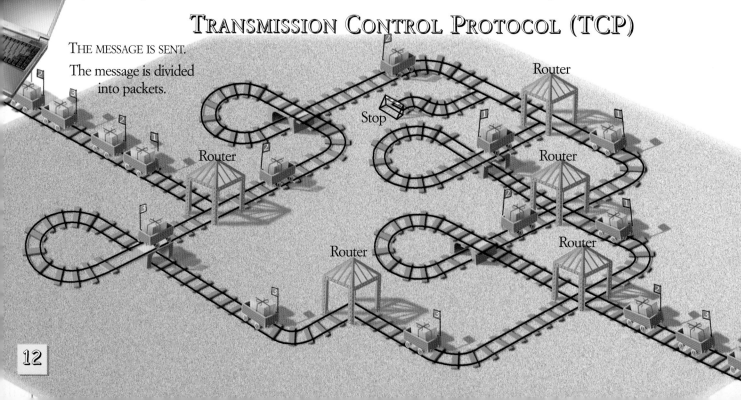

TRANSMISSION CONTROL PROTOCOL (TCP)

THE MESSAGE IS SENT.
The message is divided into packets.

Stop

Router

Router

Router

Router

Router

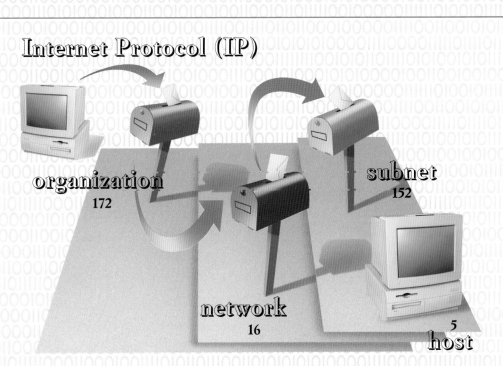

Internet Protocol (IP)

organization
172

subnet
152

network
16

host
5

Just as letters get delivered through the post office using a street address, the IP uses a simple system of numbers, from general to specific. In our example, the IP address is 172.16.152.5. First it tells the organization (172), then the network (16), the subnet (152), and finally the host computer of the user receiving the message (5).

together and are called TCP/IP. TCP/IP was invented in 1973, and it is still vital to the operation of the Internet today.

There are many other types of protocols on the Internet. Web sites use Hypertext Transfer Protocol (HTTP) to send data to personal computers. E-mails are sent using Simple Mail Transfer Protocol (SMTP). Other protocols detect network problems, transfer files, and keep track of the time. Each protocol has a different set of rules to which each participating computer must adhere. The rules for each protocol are public knowledge and usually are published in a document called a Request For Comment (RFC).

Once your computer is connected to your Internet Serice Provider (ISP), you are able to use the Internet. How does your computer in New York communicate with your friend's computer in Florida? The modem at your ISP is connected to a router. A router is a special computer that chooses the path each bit of information must take to reach its destination quickly and efficiently. A router also translates information from different networks if necessary. The router's main job is to send packets to the correct place in the correct format. Before

a packet gets to its final destination, it will travel through many routers. To save time and memory space, the router only looks at the IP portion of each packet to determine the packet's destination. Within the IP address, it identifies the network portion and decides which path to use.

For example, Router A may have connections to Routers B and C, while Router B also connects to D and Router C connects to E. If Router A gets a packet for a network on Router E, it will forward it to Router C, which will then forward the packet to Router E. Each time a router forwards a packet it is called a hop. Some parts of the Internet have many hops between them. Routers choose the best path based on the number of hops and the speed and performance of a connection. If the best route becomes unavailable, then routers choose the next-best path.

A
B
D
Hop!

Hop!
C
E

ROUTERS

THE MESSAGE IS RECEIVED.

Internetting the World

Robert Kahn and Vinton Cerf's research into computer networking was called the Internetting Research Program at ARPA. The resulting merger among diverse networks was called the Internet. They published their design for TCP in 1974, and the ARPANET switched from its earlier NCP protocol to TCP/IP in 1983.

Additional networks continued to emerge around the world. In 1975, the first links across the ocean were made through satellites. USENET, BITNET, and CSNET were new networks among universities. Because of increasing demand, the Domain Name System (DNS) was introduced in 1984, to provide an orderly system for naming the large numbers of computers on the Internet. In the 1980s, another government agency called the National Science Foundation (NSF) began building a new network for professors and students to access

computers from many universities. The NSFNET included a high-speed network, called a backbone, that connected regional networks. Gradually the computers on the ARPANET moved onto the NSFNET, and, in 1990, the ARPANET was disconnected.

Corporations like UUNET, MCI, and CERFnet began to operate commercial networks for Internet access in the late 1980s and the early 1990s. Businesses built regional networks and private backbones. They entered into agreements with each other to connect at various points, allowing access to each other's networks. Four main Network Access Points (NAPs) were built to connect these different networks together. The first of the four was the MAE East® facility in Virginia. By 1995, NSFNET no longer provided the Internet Backbone, and the Internet infrastructure was no longer under government control. Many levels of private Internet Service Providers (ISPs) had taken over the operation of the Internet infrastructure. Companies built global networks using satellite links and fiber-optic cables in the ocean. More of these networks are still being built. In 2000, there were more than seven thousand ISPs and forty different backbones in North America alone!

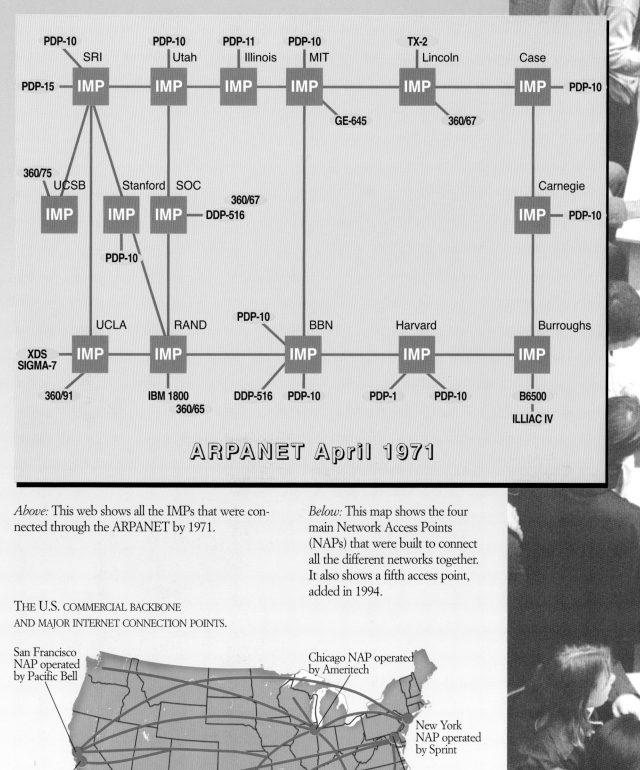

ARPANET April 1971

Above: This web shows all the IMPs that were connected through the ARPANET by 1971.

Below: This map shows the four main Network Access Points (NAPs) that were built to connect all the different networks together. It also shows a fifth access point, added in 1994.

THE U.S. COMMERCIAL BACKBONE AND MAJOR INTERNET CONNECTION POINTS.

San Francisco NAP operated by Pacific Bell

Chicago NAP operated by Ameritech

New York NAP operated by Sprint

MAE West® operated by WorldCom (added in 1994).

MAE East® facility operated by WorldCom

The Birth of the World Wide Web

By the early 1990s, the Internet had seen substantial growth, but the creation of the World Wide Web (WWW) would create even more momentum. In 1989, Tim Berners-Lee designed a system of sharing and linking files among scientists in Geneva, Switzerland. Using a special computer language called Hypertext Markup Language (HTML) and a protocol called Hypertext Transfer Protocol (HTTP), users could follow links between files. A link on one file could lead to another file on that computer or to a file on a different computer. A Web site is the collection of HTML and HTTP documents and links assembled on a single computer or set of computers. The World Wide Web became a collection of Web sites linked by computers connected to the Internet. By 1993, there were still only 150 Web sites in the world. In 2000, the number of Web sites had grown to more than seventeen million!

The World Wide Web made viewing files easier and made the Internet more useful and popular. At one of the NSF's connected sites, Marc Andreessen and others developed a more sophisticated way of viewing HTML files, called a browser. This tool read HTML files and presented them to the user on the screen. The browser was named Mosaic. Mosaic allowed computers to view HTML files easily . The browser was also the first to allow imagery to be included in the hypertext links. In 1994, Marc Andreessen and Jim Clark produced a more advanced browser called Netscape. Microsoft soon produced its own browser, called Internet Explorer. Consumer use of the Internet began to grow rapidly because browsers were easy to use, computers were more common, and Internet access was widely available.

The uses of the World Wide Web expand daily. New industries emerged in the middle to late 1990s as more people joined the Internet community. Companies like Amazon.com, Yahoo!, and America Online grew at tremendous rates. The WWW now includes sites for businesses, education, government, entertainment, and much more. The Internet infrastructure continues to grow to accommodate new applications, or software that allows a user to perform a certain task. Companies that own backbones are called carriers. The large carriers, like WorldCom and AT&T, are building larger and faster backbone networks to allow easy use of video and other new technology.

Right: This is the original diagram by Tim Berners-Lee showing his proposal of a system that would allow files to be shared and to be linked between various computers. Using a special computer language called Hypertext Markup Language (HTML) and a protocol called Hypertext Transfer Protocol (HTTP), users could follow links between files. The system was useful because of the flexible methods of searching. One user could end up with the same answer even if the search method or path followed was not the same as every other user's.

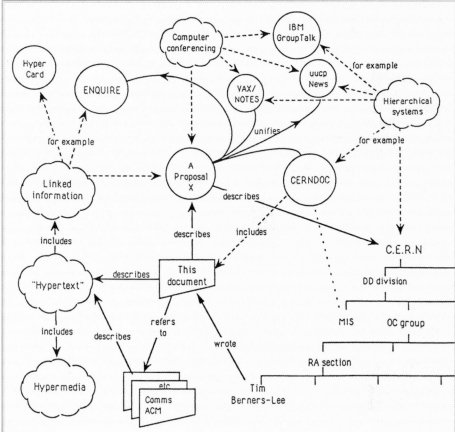

Left: Hundreds of Internet companies sprang up after the World Wide Web community became increasingly larger.

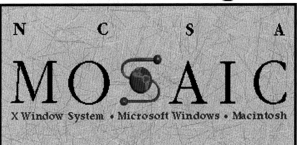

Right: Browsers like Netscape, Internet Explorer, and Mosaic made the Internet more user friendly.

Top Left: A CERN laboratory in Geneva, Switzerland, where the foundation for the World Wide Web was built by Tim Berners-Lee.

Bottom Left: Tim Berners-Lee with his NeXTcube Turbo, the workstation invented by Steve Jobs, who was the founder of Apple. Berners-Lee used this computer as he expanded the uses of the World Wide Web.

Getting Connected

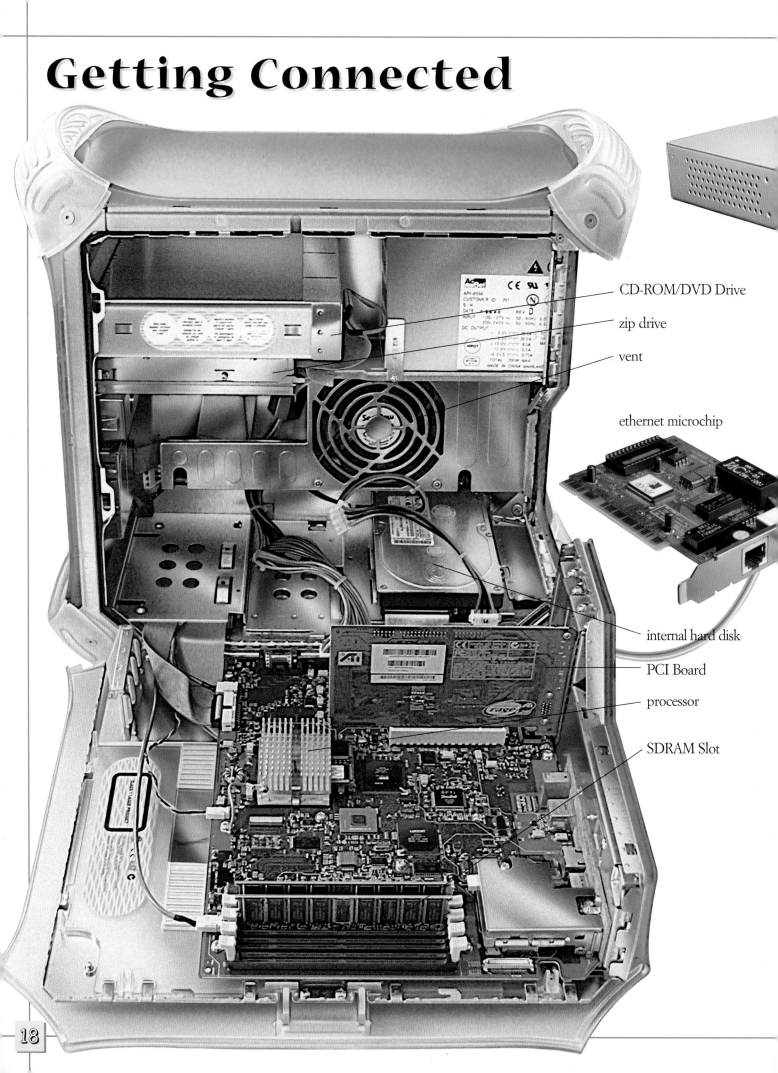

CD-ROM/DVD Drive

zip drive

vent

ethernet microchip

internal hard disk

PCI Board

processor

SDRAM Slot

hub

ethernet microchip

twisted
pair
copper
cable

How does the average person connect to the Internet? Most home computers use modems to connect to the Internet. Modem stands for modulator-demodulator, and it turns digital data on the computer into analog data that can be sent through telephone lines. Analog data is measured by varying electrical force, or voltage, or by varying sound frequency. A receiving modem measures voltage levels and translates the measurements into bits of data. The connection process begins by starting a software program on a computer. The software gives commands to the computer's modem to dial a telephone number at the ISP. This telephone number is connected to another modem at the ISP's data center.

Once the modems connect, they begin a handshake process. The two modems agree on how quickly they will send each other information and which packet format to use. They do this by using the Point to Point Protocol (PPP). Most modems will send from 28,000 to 128,000 bits every second. After a few seconds, the home modem and the ISP's modem have shared PPP information and have established a connection. The ISP then assigns your computer a temporary IP address to use on the Internet.

Ethernet is a type of local network for the transmission, or sending, of data. It was developed by Xerox, Intel, and Digital and connects computers through chips or boards inserted into the computer. They are tied to hubs and other connectors by copper cable. Ethernet is the type of local-area network (LAN) used by most small-and medium-size businesses.

Your modem is able to send its PPP information because it has a physical connection to the telephone company. Each telephone or modem requires two pieces of thin, copper wire to send and to receive information. The wires run to the basement of your apartment building or up the telephone pole outside your house. They connect into a series of telephone machines, called repeaters, which reproduce the analog signal along many more wires before it reaches the telephone company's central office. The central office sends the signal to the modem at the ISP. The ISP also has connections to the telephone company. Once your signal reaches the ISP, both computers share PPP information, your computer gets an IP address, and you are now connected to the Internet.

There are many other ways to make a local Internet connection. Some other ways of connecting to the Internet, like Ethernet or Integrated Switched Digital Network (ISDN), don't need to change data from analog to digital. Ethernet and ISDN are additional protocols that send data quickly between computers. Some areas offer ISDN, Digital Subscriber Loop (DSL), or access through cable modems. These methods allow the computer to communicate at higher speeds and don't need to translate from digital to analog. DSL and ISDN use standard telephone lines to connect. Cable connections use a single, thicker cable, called a coaxial cable, to carry more information.

The Internet Backbone

An ISP in Florida and your ISP are connected to each other through the Internet Backbone. There are actually many high-speed networks that make up the Internet Backbone. Unlike your modem at home, the Internet Backbone is extremely fast. In order to be so fast, the Internet needs a lot of bandwidth to send billions of bits around the world. Bandwidth is a measure of how many bits can be sent each second. One Megabit per second (Mbps) is one million bits of data sent every second. This page has about 250 words and 1,500 letters and spaces. That adds up to 96,000 bits. If you had a 10-Megabit Ethernet, you could send this page 104 times in one second. The Internet Backbone is even faster. On the Internet Backbone, you could send this page more than 100,000 times in one second!

The Internet Backbone uses fiber-optic cables, which are very thin strands of glass, to send data. Fiber-optic equipment uses lasers to transmit data with pulses of light. These strands of glass are actually stronger than steel! There are very long fibers, which are up to 15 miles (24 km) long, laid beneath cities to connect networks to each other. They are often buried next to railroads or under streets in cities. Between England and the rest of Europe, fiber-optic cables are run inside the Eurotunnel. When workers need to repair the fiber strands, they either have to go down the manholes or dig holes in the ground to get to the cables.

Fiber-optic cables are used to connect many countries around the world. Very long cables are laid and are buried in the ocean floor. These oceanic cables are covered with special metal casings to protect them from saltwater corrosion and objects in the ocean. There are cables that connect North America to Japan, and cables that connect the United States to Europe. Several large companies, including Global Crossing, are building new fiber-optic networks to add more capacity for global back-bones.

Other types of backbone connections include satellite and radio links. Satellites orbiting Earth provide connections for many long-distance links. An earth station is a site on Earth that communicates with the satellites. The earth station sends the signal to the satellite, and the satellite relays the signal to an earth station at a particular destination. Satellite links are slower than fiber-optic links, and satellite links sometimes experience problems caused by environmental events, like sunspots.

U.S.A.

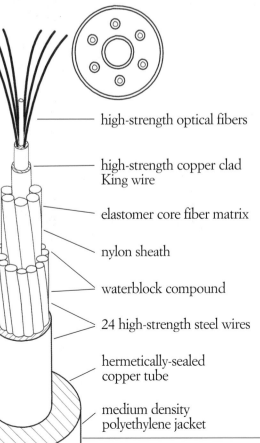

high-strength optical fibers

high-strength copper clad King wire

elastomer core fiber matrix

nylon sheath

waterblock compound

24 high-strength steel wires

hermetically-sealed copper tube

medium density polyethylene jacket

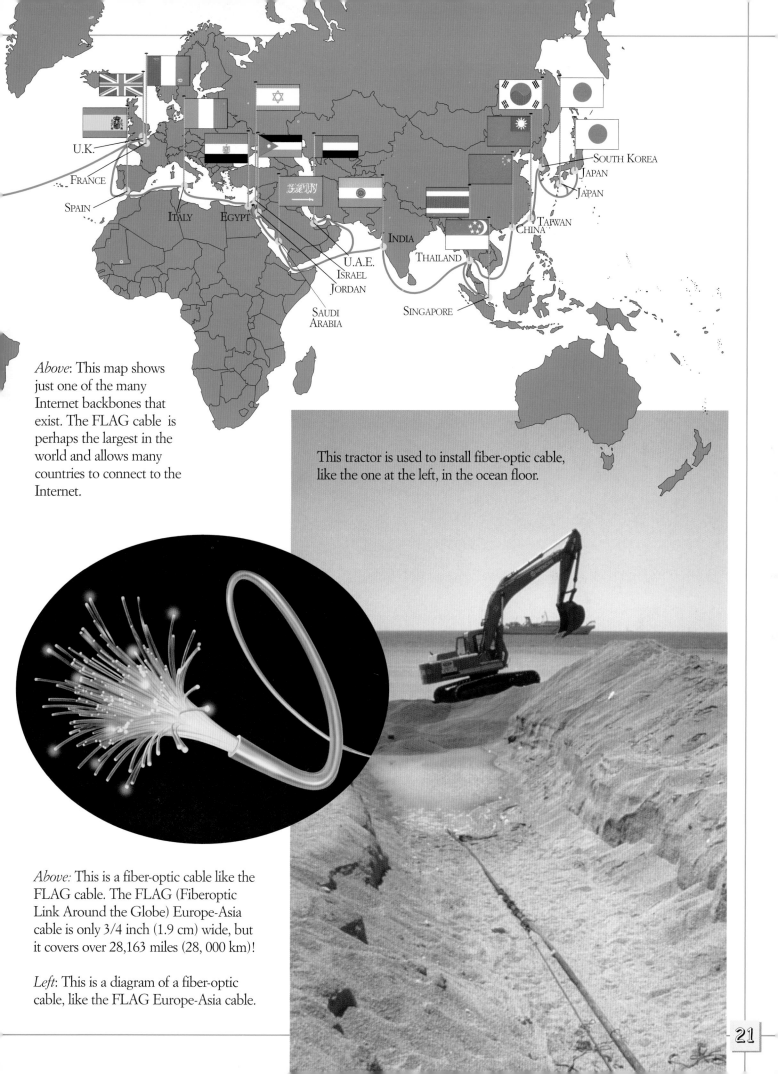

U.K.

FRANCE

SPAIN

ITALY   EGYPT

INDIA

U.A.E.
ISRAEL
JORDAN

SAUDI
ARABIA

THAILAND

SINGAPORE

CHINA

TAIWAN

SOUTH KOREA

JAPAN

JAPAN

Above: This map shows just one of the many Internet backbones that exist. The FLAG cable is perhaps the largest in the world and allows many countries to connect to the Internet.

This tractor is used to install fiber-optic cable, like the one at the left, in the ocean floor.

Above: This is a fiber-optic cable like the FLAG cable. The FLAG (Fiberoptic Link Around the Globe) Europe-Asia cable is only 3/4 inch (1.9 cm) wide, but it covers over 28,163 miles (28, 000 km)!

Left: This is a diagram of a fiber-optic cable, like the FLAG Europe-Asia cable.

Managing the Internet

The Internet is a vast collection of networks. People use it 24 hours a day, 365 days a year all around the world. With millions of connected computers using hundreds of different protocols, maintaining the Internet is very complicated. No single organization oversees the entire Internet. Each carrier, ISP, or business builds and manages its own infrastructure, or internal workings, but several groups work together on the basic technical needs of the Internet as a whole.

Below: The World Wide Web Consortium develops international standards for the Internet.

Most of the computer networks on the Internet are carefully monitored in various Network Operations Centers (NOCs). An NOC receives information from network computers, like routers and servers, that identify problems with network connections and protocols. Routing protocols allow the Internet to send traffic around problems, but there are many other types of possible problems that aren't easily fixed. Cables buried in the street or in the ocean are occasionally damaged. To fix a fiber-optic cable break, highly trained workers must splice, or join, the cables by carefully merging the glass strands together in a portable oven. Other events also cause disruptions on the Internet. In 1995, a bonfire in Minnesota melted some fiber-optic cables used for regional Internet connections. The next year, several Internet Service Providers (ISPs) lost network connections for hours because of a router problem.

Below: This is the logo for the Internet Assigned Numbers Authority.

The rapid growth of the Internet has required some form of organization to control and to manage it. The Internet Society (ISOC) is an international organization that leads the development of new standards and confronts global Internet issues. Other groups handle domain names for Web sites and IP addresses. The Domain Name System (DNS) is a directory of names used for locating computers on the Internet. Some examples of domain names are *cnn.com* and *isoc.org*. Each domain name must be registered with an official body to ensure each domain name is unique. The Internet Assigned Numbers Authority (IANA) is responsible for creating new domain names and for governing the groups that reg-

Internet Assigned Numbers Authority

Left: Ken Hansen, director of corporate development at NeuStar Inc., talks about the impact of new Domain Name Suffixes (DNS) at the conclusion of the Internet Corporation for Assigned Names and Numbers (ICANN) annual meeting November 16, 2000, in the Marina del Rey area of Los Angeles. ICANN selected seven new DNS categories, including .aero, .coop, .info, .museum, .name and .pro.

ister the names. The registering is handled by groups like Reseaux IP Europeens (RIPE) in Europe and the Asia-Pacific Network Information Center (APNIC) in Asia. The World Wide Web Consortium (W3C) provides international leadership to develop new standards and technologies on the World Wide Web.

Right: This is an image of the International World Wide Web Conference Committee logo.

Right: CERN General Director General, L. Maiani, signs the letter of intent to establish a regional computer center in Pakistan on September 15, 2000, during the visit of Professor Atta-ur Rahman, minister of Science and Technology of Pakistan.

E-mail

E-mail is one of the oldest uses of the Internet. It was invented by Ray Tomlinson in 1971. To send an e-mail, you first need an e-mail address. An e-mail address has two parts: a user name and a domain name. A sample address is *christopher.columbus@newworld.com*. The first part, *christopher.columbus*, identifies the user of the e-mail address. The second part, following the @ symbol, *newworld.com*, is the domain name and identifies where the mail should be sent to reach the user.

Let's follow the path of an e-mail sent to Christopher Columbus. Once you've entered the e-mail address and typed your message, you select the "send" button on your e-mail software. This tells

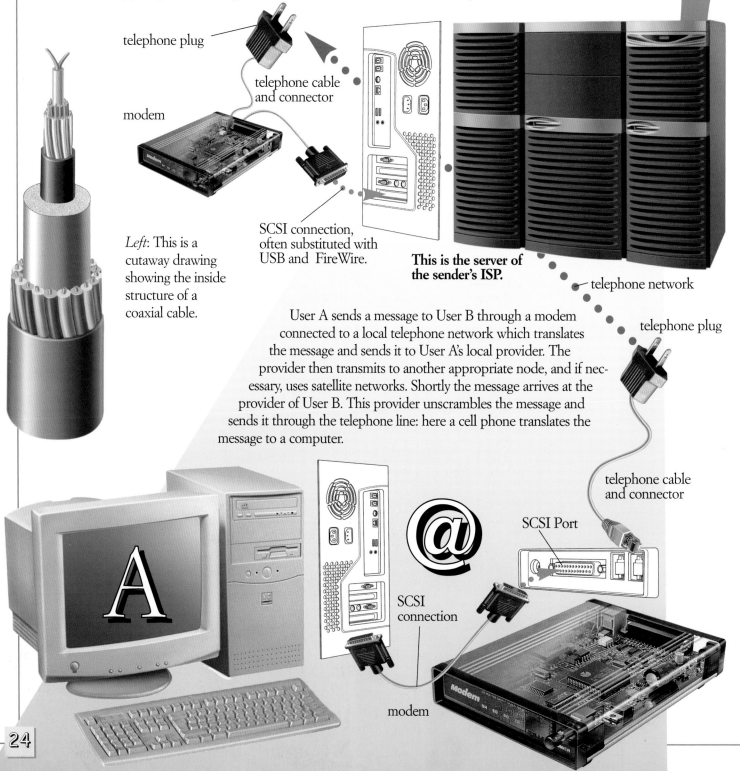

telephone plug

telephone cable and connector

modem

Left: This is a cutaway drawing showing the inside structure of a coaxial cable.

SCSI connection, often substituted with USB and FireWire.

This is the server of the sender's ISP.

telephone network

telephone plug

User A sends a message to User B through a modem connected to a local telephone network which translates the message and sends it to User A's local provider. The provider then transmits to another appropriate node, and if necessary, uses satellite networks. Shortly the message arrives at the provider of User B. This provider unscrambles the message and sends it through the telephone line: here a cell phone translates the message to a computer.

telephone cable and connector

SCSI Port

SCSI connection

modem

Telecommunications Satellite

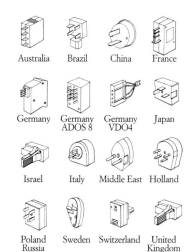

Australia Brazil China France

Germany Germany ADOS 8 Germany VDO4 Japan

Israel Italy Middle East Holland

Poland Russia Sweden Switzerland United Kingdom

Above: Plugs are not the same in every country, but they all provide power to computers in the same way.

your computer to change the letters and the numbers of your message into binary ones and zeros so your computer can send the e-mail. Your computer puts your text into a packet and adds protocol information. Your computer uses a special e-mail protocol like Post Office Protocol 3 (POP3) or IMAP. Before the message can be sent, your computer uses POP3 to verify that you have an account on that server. If you're using a modem with Point to Point Protocol (PPP), your computer will add POP3 information, then IP information, then PPP information to the packet before it transmits the bits through your telephone line to your ISP.

The e-mail packet is sent to your ISP's email server. Once your mail server receives the message, it will communicate with the mail server at the domain in the address, *newworld.com*. Your packet is routed like any other Internet traffic. The electrical pulses travel through all the cables and the computers that connect your ISP to Christopher's ISP. Your e-mail may be broken into several packets, and it will probably travel through several offices containing many routers and switches. Once all the packets reach the mail server at your friend's ISP, Transmission Control Protocol (TCP) reassembles them and forwards the message to the e-mail software on the server.

This is the server of the destination's provider.

telephone plug

telephone line

modem

Once the message reaches the server, it is saved in a file until Christopher connects to the Internet and accesses his e-mail. Christopher's computer also uses a protocol like POP3 to communicate with his ISP's e-mail server. The e-mail server sends the message to Christopher's computer using TCP/IP, and Christopher's computer reassembles the packets into one message. His e-mail software translates the bits of ones and zeros into text on the screen. Christopher can then read the e-mail message.

telephone plug

hub

modem

B

@

Local networks work with computers of various types.

A cellular telephone connects to a portable computer.

Using The World Wide Web

The World Wide Web is a collection of files spread across many computers around the world. These files are on computers called Web servers. The files can contain text, pictures, sounds, graphics, or anything else that developers can create. The files can also contain small programs that perform a specific task, like hosting a chess game. The term "surfing the Net" was coined because Web pages contain links that let users move quickly from one site to another. When users click on new links before the old links finish loading, they are said to be "surfing" the Web. The universal format of Internet protocols allows a computer anywhere in the world to view Web pages through the Internet.

To use the World Wide Web, you need a browser. Two popular browsers today are Internet Explorer and Netscape Navigator. A browser is a software program that translates data coded with Hypertext Markup Language (HTML) and displays the information on your computer screen. HTML files contain instructions, or tags, that tell the browser how to display the data. For example if there is an HTML code of <P>, this indicates the start of a paragraph and tells the browser to add an indent. The HTML file also may contain references to other files, and have links to reach other sites. To see a Web page's HTML tags, try selecting View Page Source or View Frame Source from the menus of your browser.

To view a Web page on a browser, you must have its Uniform Resource Locator, or URL. The URL identifies a particular computer and a service for accessing the data on that computer. Services are different ways to retrieve information, like the World Wide Web or File Transfers. The host includes a domain name and identifies the Web server for the site. One example of a URL is *http://www.louvre.fr*. This identifies the Web site for the Louvre Museum in Paris. The service is the WWW, and the protocol used for World Wide Web communication is Hypertext Transfer Protocol (HTTP). URLs can be used for other services besides the World Wide Web, including e-mail and non-HTTP file transfers.

To visit the Louvre Web site, you must enter the URL for the site into your browser. Your ISP's Domain Name Resolver will translate the host name portion of the URL into the IP address

of the Web server at the Louvre. Your computer will build a packet with HTTP information, IP information, including the IP address of the Web server, and your local protocol information. Then transmit the data on your local connection. The Web server opens a connection with your computer, allows your browser to read the HTML instructions, and displays the file specified in the URL. Some types of files, like pictures or song clips, take a longer time to load because the file was broken into many packets, and they must be reassembled before it can be displayed. Loading files could also take longer if many Web surfers are accessing the same Web server at the same time. Each time you select another link, additional HTTP packets must be sent to the server to read the tags on the selected HTML file. If the main Web page at *http://www.louvre.fr* contained a hyperlink called Mona Lisa, and the HTML file for that link included a reference to a picture of the *Mona Lisa*, your browser would display the *Mona Lisa* on your computer if you clicked on the link with your mouse.

Each picture here is an ex-ample of pages viewable on the Web. Depending on the type of applets each page runs, some have sound, moving images, or links that allow the user to navigate the site easily. Internet sites can be educational, like these museum and cultural sites, or for entertainment, like the interactive game Web site, above.

Above: Each of these images is a screen capture of an educational Web site's home page. The home page is usually the first page of any site a user visits. This page then provides the user with a directory of the kind of information accessible on the site.

Other Ways to Use the Internet

There are many other ways to use the Internet in addition to e-mail and to viewing HTML files. Programming languages like Java and ActiveX enhance Web pages by adding movement and short programs. Java is used to create small programs called applets that can be run on any type of computer. Online Internet games would not be possible with just HTML files. Many interactive Web pages use applets to launch graphics. The number of uses for applets is limited only by the imagination of the developers.

A growing use for the Internet is to make telephone calls. The call works much differently than does a regular telephone call, and there is actually no telephone involved! The computers making the call must have special sound cards with microphones. Computer software converts the sound of a voice into binary digits and compresses the amount of data by using mathematical formulas. The packets with the converted voice data are sent through the Internet using TCP/IP and are reassembled at the destination. The other computer decodes that digital data into voice sounds and plays the sounds on a speaker.

Internet users can also communicate immediately with others through Internet Relay Chat (IRC) or Instant Messaging (IM). Instead of accessing e-mail by downloading files, IRC users display a window that represents an IRC channel. Each person that accesses the channel can enter text that is seen by all the other people looking at that channel at the same time.

Users can listen to music and can view video through the Internet as well. MP3 is a standard application for encoding music in digital files. The files can then be played through the Internet or sent through TCP/IP to a friend. Streaming media technologies allow audio and video to be converted to digital bits, compressed, and sent through the Internet.

There are many other ways to use the Internet. Most companies have a presence on the World Wide Web. Shoppers can buy items from online Web stores like Amazon.com. People can access news through text, sound, and video clips. Students can learn about new subjects by viewing Web pages about history, science, or art. More information is stored on the Internet every day, and new ways to share it constantly emerge.

The Internet is not just for emailing, looking up information about the planets, or finding a favorite recipe. It has become the world's largest shopping mall as well. Millions of people use the Web to buy and sell goods every day.

B2B

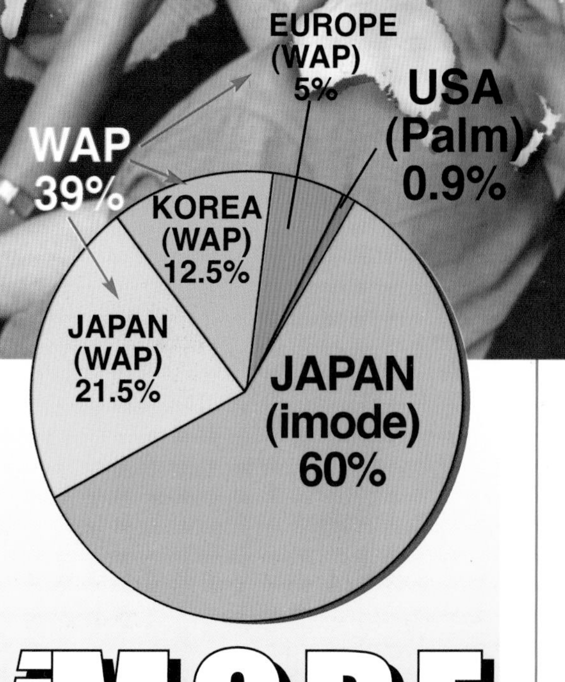

Business to Business, or B2B, is another Internet trend. Also called e-business, B2B simply means that businesses on the Web are buying or selling services with other businesses instead of the consumer. It is not a term that refers only to businesses online, but the Web provides these businesses, such as software companies, with a whole new market in which to buy and to sell goods and services.

Right: The pie graph shows the percentage of people in various countries that are using wireless Internet technologies.

MP3

MP3 is another new use of the Internet. MP3 is a system that compresses, or makes a music file smaller, without hurting the quality of the sound. A song from a CD could take more than two hours to download. The MP3 allows a song to be downloaded in seconds without your ear hearing a difference in quality. With MP3 a user can search for and download almost any song.

EUROPE (WAP) 5%

USA (Palm) 0.9%

WAP 39%

KOREA (WAP) 12.5%

JAPAN (WAP) 21.5%

JAPAN (imode) 60%

iMODE

Since Mari Matsunaga invented iMODE, there have been more than 16 million subscribers. In Japan iMODE has been developed as the first complete wireless internet service. iMODE works through packet switching and is always on as long as the hand set can access the radio signal from the provider. The main uses for iMODE right now are e-mail, stock trading, online banking, games, and other general uses.

Security and Privacy

The Internet is open to everyone. With this openness, there is a risk that some people will use their Internet connection to cause damage. Some people write programs called viruses that can cause damage to computers by deleting files or programs that computers need to operate. One virus in 2000 was called the Love Letter virus, because it was sent as an e-mail with the subject heading that read, "I love you." Another potentially harmful program is called a worm. A worm replicates itself from computer to computer and infects files. In 1988, a worm program affected 6,000 of the 60,000 computers then connected to the Internet. Some people also gain access to networks through routers or servers attached to telephone lines and can cause the network to stop working by resetting systems or by changing configurations.

There are ways to protect against viruses and network intrusion. A system called a firewall provides some protection to computer networks. A firewall can be a single computer with special software or several computers and routers working together to protect the network. The firewall is attached between the network and the Internet. It looks at packets sent into the network and decides whether they should be allowed to pass. The firewall can be configured to block particular protocols or IP addresses. If a company wants to block all packets from a particular network, the firewall is configured to deny any packets that contain the IP addresses of that network.

Another form of virus protection is a software program called a virus scanner. Scanners check files and eliminate viruses before they can damage any other files.

Right: A major concern on the Internet is privacy. Since the birth of computer networks, there has always been the threat that a hacker could access private, or confidential, information about a person, a company, or an agency. Sometimes a hacker just wants to cause mischief, but other times stolen information can be used to conduct crimes. Whatever the reason, secrity is a top priority on many Web sites. This image is from a press conference held in Wooodbridge High School in California. These four teens tell how they broke into a computer pay network. After the FBI confiscated their home computers, the boys said that they were unaware that they had cut into a commercial computer network. Left to right: Wayne Correia, 17, Gary Knutson, 15, Greg Knutson, 14, and David Hill, 17, tell their story.

Another concern in using the Internet is the accessibility of inappropriate content. Parents and teachers often choose to block out certain sites so they cannot be accessed from a particular computer. The openness of the Internet and the many different users means that there is a lot of different information and material out there on the Web. Users need to be aware of this and carefully select the sites they wish to see.

Privacy is another large concern in the open Internet society. Public records are available on the Internet. Some Internet companies track how people use their Web sites through computer records and files called cookies. A cookie can record which sites someone visits and can identify which parts of a site are used. Data is often sent through the Internet without any protection. If someone bought a jar of pickles with a credit card and paid through the Internet, his credit card number could potentially be stolen when the payment was made. To protect secret information on computers and across networks, data is frequently encrypted. With encryption, data is scrambled at the sending

computer and unscrambled only when the data reaches the other end. Both computers must share the same key to encode and to decode the message, or they must use public key cryptography and agree on a method for encoding their information. A complicated mathematical formula is used to encrypt data.

Above: This image represents a computer virus. Viruses are programs that damage the user's computer by deleting files or by causing things not to work properly.

The Semantic Web

Already in the works is a new use of the Internet, called the Semantic Web. This will utilize artificial intelligence technology to improve a computer's ability to search and access information. The Semantic Web will be a far more sophisticated and accurate tool than the World Wide Web by itself, allowing users and computers to work together more efficiently.

Here is just one example of how the Semantic Web will be used. With the Semantic Web, if a person makes reservations for an extended trip abroad, the airlines, the hotels, the soccer stadiums, and so on will return confirmations with semantic markup. This markup information will tell all the schedules to load directly into your date book and all the expenses to load directly into your accounting program, no matter what semantics-enabled software you use. A person will no longer need to sort through all the information on a Web site or in an e-mail and then input it into their own systems, or write it on their calendars. This is pretty amazing stuff!

The task at hand right now is for designers to add logic to the World Wide Web. Rules must be added that allow the Semantic Web to make decisions, to choose a course of action, and to answer unknown questions without getting stuck in a loop if something unanswerable comes up.

The real power of the Semantic Web will come when there are more software agents that will collect, process, and share information gathered on the Web with other programs. Agents will go out to find the information a user requests and report back with the answer along with proof of the validity of the information. The agent will load the information into the appropriate software on a user's system and include any warning notes or things that should be verified. Different agents will be able to speak with each other by exchanging the rules they have for meaning and thereby gain access to a wide range of information.

The projected abilities of the Semantic Web are too general to be

Right: This diagram shows a scenario where Lucy's agent needs to track down a physical therapy office for her mother that meets certain qualifications and has appointment times that fit with her and her brother's schedules.

The Semantic Web will change the way we use the Internet. Just as the World Wide Web revolutionized the world of information, the Semantic Web's impact cannot yet be imagined.

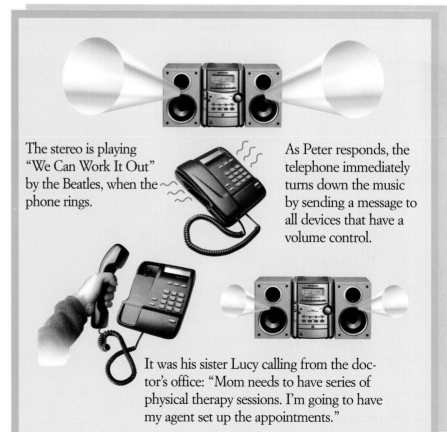

The stereo is playing "We Can Work It Out" by the Beatles, when the phone rings.

As Peter responds, the telephone immediately turns down the music by sending a message to all devices that have a volume control.

It was his sister Lucy calling from the doctor's office: "Mom needs to have series of physical therapy sessions. I'm going to have my agent set up the appointments."

thought about in terms of solving one key problem. Nonetheless it will have uses we haven't dreamed of and enough power and flexibility to revolutionize the way we access information.

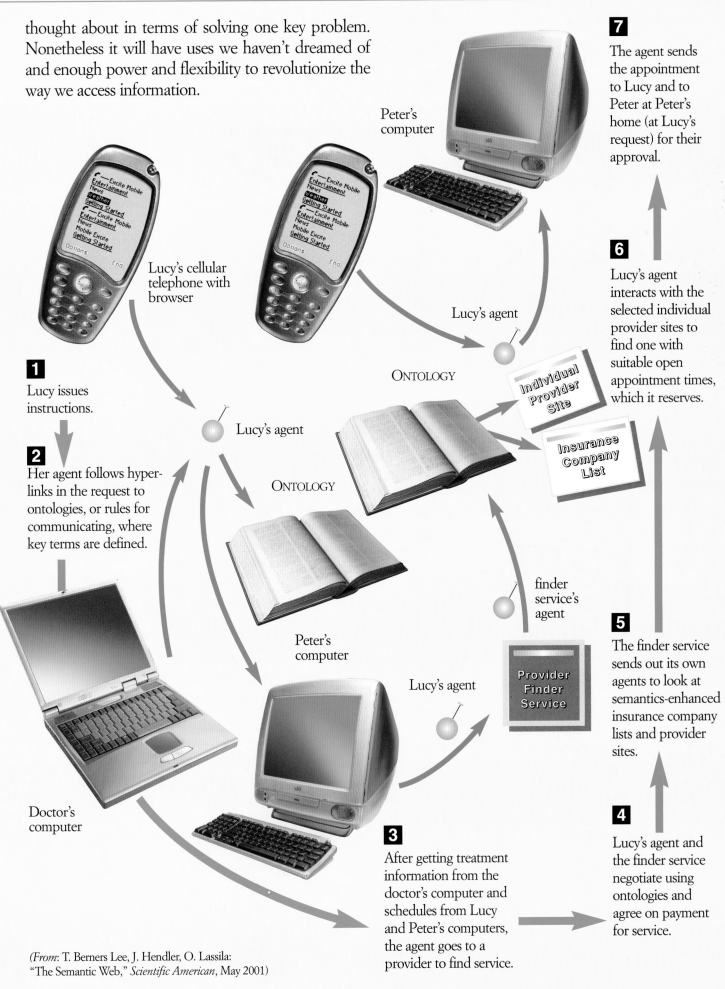

Peter's computer

Lucy's cellular telephone with browser

Lucy's agent

1 Lucy issues instructions.

2 Her agent follows hyperlinks in the request to ontologies, or rules for communicating, where key terms are defined.

ONTOLOGY

ONTOLOGY

Peter's computer

Lucy's agent

Doctor's computer

3 After getting treatment information from the doctor's computer and schedules from Lucy and Peter's computers, the agent goes to a provider to find service.

finder service's agent

Provider Finder Service

4 Lucy's agent and the finder service negotiate using ontologies and agree on payment for service.

5 The finder service sends out its own agents to look at semantics-enhanced insurance company lists and provider sites.

Individual Provider Site

Insurance Company List

6 Lucy's agent interacts with the selected individual provider sites to find one with suitable open appointment times, which it reserves.

7 The agent sends the appointment to Lucy and to Peter at Peter's home (at Lucy's request) for their approval.

(*From*: T. Berners Lee, J. Hendler, O. Lassila: "The Semantic Web," *Scientific American*, May 2001)

Cultural and Economic Impact

A case full of rare books (*above*), the home page of the Louvre (*below*), the Library of Congress in Washington, D.C. (*bottom center*), and the British Library in London (*far right*) are all major cultural institutions that have been impacted by the Internet.

It is difficult to overstate the Internet's impact on many areas of society. It has been more quickly adopted than has any other technology, including the telephone, the radio, or the television. The economic impact has been incredible in its directions, both up and down. Entire new markets and business models have emerged online. Companies like eBay and Amazon.com gain all of their revenue from Internet transactions. The companies that build Internet computers and software, such as Microsoft, Oracle, and Cisco, have experienced incredible growth, and many other companies have used the Internet to become more efficient. As companies rush to build Web sites and networks, they must purchase network equipment and software and must hire highly skilled people to install and maintain the expensive systems. There aren't enough information technology professionals and programmers to fill all the available positions. Starting with Netscape, the stock market has generated great amounts of wealth by increasing the value of Internet companies. Many Internet technology companies use stock to attract new employees.

The growth of the Internet also has had an impact on politics and government. On the Internet, people can send information to any part of the world in less than one second. It is very easy to share all types of information. The Internet also has no national boundaries. This has increased interactions between people in different countries, and it has had a melting-pot effect. Official boundaries between countries are becoming less significant as more financial transactions and social interactions take place on the Internet. Governments have had to adapt to the new technology. Governments must cooperate to develop rules that will allow the Internet to continue to flourish across international borders. The Internet Society works to increase Internet access for poor countries. Crime-fighting units and legislatures have developed new techniques and laws to combat cybercrime, or crimes that take place on computer networks.

We also have seen an effect on culture. The Internet allows new forms of entertainment, like interactive video games. People make friends around the world on the Internet. Movies like *You've got Mail* and *The Matrix* show that the Internet is a significant influence on our daily lives and on our imaginations. It has changed the way we shop, play, and communicate. Anyone can add his or her own collection of text and graphics and contribute to the content of the World Wide Web.

From the nation's classrooms to museums like the Louvre to the Library of Congress, the Internet has changed the way we live as a society. The Internet has caused an information explosion, in which anyone can access almost any information from anyplace on the globe.

The Future of the Internet

The future expectation of the Internet is that it will continue to grow. In 2000, there were 300 million people connected to the Internet. By January 2001, there were 407 million, and in just a few years, the number of people connected will rise into the billions. The number of computers on the Internet will also continue to increase. Soon normal appliances like refrigerators could be connected to the Internet. It will be possible for your refrigerator to know its own contents, suggest recipes, and order groceries through the Internet. Other types of devices specifically designed for Internet use also may become more popular.

The Internet infrastructure will continue to expand and to improve. Many companies are building larger fiber-optic networks, which will support higher speeds for transmitting information. Newer methods of connecting to the Internet, like DSL and cable modems, will become more popular as more areas have available high-speed access. Two groups are already researching new ways to increase the speed and the capacity of the Internet. Internet 2 is a project joined by more than 120 research institutions. Internet 2 is trying to develop ultra-high-speed technologies and new network services that eventually will be used by the public Internet. The Next Generation Internet (NGI) is a U.S. government project to increase Internet access speed by 100 times.

The Internet will even expand beyond Earth. NASA's Jet Propulsion Laboratory (JPL) is developing new protocols for network communications between planets. This new network, called InterPlaNet (IPN), will provide a communications backbone in space to support exploration of the planets.

The Internet will continue to grow and to spread to every area of the globe. Wireless access will enable users to bring the Internet everywhere and have

Below:
Lightwave networks will combine, amplify, switch, and restore optical signals without converting them to an electronic transmission for processing. A dense wavelength division multiplexer (DWDM) will take different wavelengths of light and will place them on a single fiber connection. An optical amplifier will boost the signals. An optical switch will route different wavelengths, and an amplifier that regenerates a signal will restore the timing and shape of the pulses in the signal before a demultiplexer separates each wavelength and sends telephone calls, computer files. or video to their recipients.

From: Gary Stix: "The Triumph of the Light," *Scientific American*, January 2001.

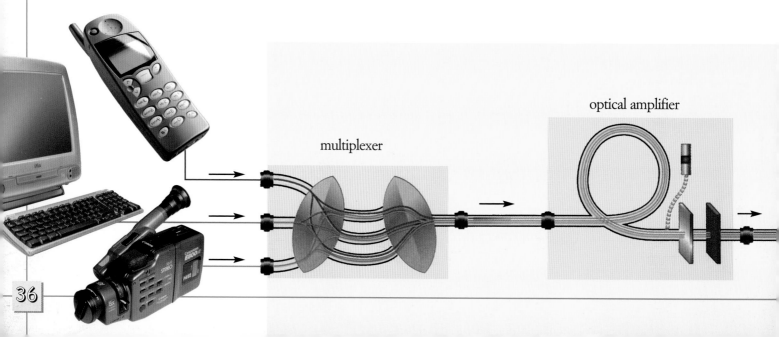

multiplexer

optical amplifier

Left: An optical multiplexer, a component of an optical packet router, sends four incoming wavelengths to two output ports.

The uses of the Internet are only limited by the imagination of the user. As more people get connected, whole industries will crop up to meet the need for fasterconnections that can handle more volume. From computers, cameras, and cell phones to space stations, automobiles and kitchen appliances, there will be almost nothing that cannot be plugged in and used online.

constant access to information and to communication. A wireless connection is mobile because there are no cables that connect the computer to the Internet. Computers will improve in speed and in power to provide faster access to an ever-increasing array of data. Artificial intelligence will create better search engines and online tools like digital personal assistants.

Brand-new technologies and applications will emerge that we can't even imagine today. The potential of the Internet is limitless, and young people like you will shape the future of this precious resource.

optical switches

optical signal regeneration

demultiplexer

Interview with Vinton Cerf

Interviewer (I): **What are your forecasts for the growth and saturation for wireless Internet devices?**

Vinton Cerf (VC): There are hundreds of millions of wireless devices in use today, including mobile telephones, TV remote controllers, wireless local area networks, and so on. Many, but by no means all, of these devices are Internet-enabled (or IP-enabled, to be precise). Today's mobile phones provide relatively low data-rate access to Internet, but this is expected to evolve from about 10,000 bits per second today to millions of bits per second in the next few years. Already there are wireless local area networks that support Internet access at rates of 11 million bits per second.

If we were speaking to each other in 1900, instead of in 2000, you might be asking me questions about 'horseless carriages' and I would be saying to you that the term 'horseless carriage' does not do justice to what we are working with here. What we have here is an automobile. The way in which we've viewed the World Wide Web up until now is probably too confining. Let's take an example of computers that understand our speech. Today's speech-activated computers typically do not understand the terms call and home, but more advanced computers will. Nuance and Speechworks are two examples of companies developing software that allows computers to understand spoken speech in a variety of languages. The speech-understanding capability will make the mobile telephone device far more useful than it is in its current mode of operation. One of the most exciting new developments in the Internet is the voice-enabled Internet, which enables people to browse the Internet using spoken commands and inputs.

It is anticipated that there will be more wireless devices. There could be as many as 1.5 billion wireless, Internet-enabled telephones by the year 2006—more than the anticipated number of personal computers and laptops. There may be different ways to use laptops and personal digital assistants, but we may find that each device has its strengths and its limitations.

What we need, and do not yet have, are protocols that will explain to the server computers what the end device is capable of doing. For example, by telling the server how much memory is available, it may be concluded that attachments to messages need to be kept at the server and not delivered to the low-capacity end device. The server will want to know what protocols and formats it can use to communicate with the end device so it can adapt its presentations.

I: **Is there development along these lines?**

VC: One of the most important new developments in the Internet Protocol world is session initiation protocol (SIP), which is used to set up Internet-telephony calls over the Internet. SIP will be used as a general purpose tool for mediating client/server and peer interactions. Peer relationships are pivotal to the new application protocols. SIP works both ways.

I: **What do you think will be the major Internet applications down the road ?**

VC: Conventional kinds of entertainment have turned out to be very hard to implement on the Internet. There has been no significant penetration except for one-way audio (radio) offered by some 15,000 sources around the world. Digital broadcast satellite will be as good a way as any to distribute Internet data packets to a large number of receivers at one time permitting one to listen to an Internet radio station while driving all the way across the United States, for example. There are an increasing number of Internet-enabled appliances finding their way into the market and onto the Internet. One of the more innovative is an Internet-enabled picture frame that simply downloads images from a predetermined Web site and displays them in rotation. I do believe that other forms of entertainment will find their way onto the Internet, particularly as group interaction becomes better supported and attracts more players.

I: **How would you define an Internet appliance?**

VC: Any device that is on the Internet, even things that

you don't normally consider to be a computer, can be an Internet appliance, such as a telephone, a refrigerator, or even a bathroom scale! The prototype Internet refrigerators have liquid crystal, touch-sensitive displays. There's a good chance that the refrigerators will have barcode scanners to track their own contents. This may allow the refrigerator of the future to inventory itself and look around on the Net for recipes that use the items in the refrigerator.

The idea that there is software doing things for you in the background while you are doing something else, is very interesting to me. We already have the infrastructure out there, so you can start thinking about new applications that can add value to existing services. There are going to be lots of opportunities. The most astonishing ones will turn products into services. For example, Procter & Gamble might develop a Web site so that if you get a stain on your shirt (ketchup for example), there will be a way to learn how to use their soap to eliminate the stain. The Web site could even send instructions to your Internet-enabled washing machine to set it up to use the soap properly. The

result: a box of soap has been turned into a service!

I: **You've spoken of the possibility of an interplanetary Internet (IPN). What's the future of this idea?**
VC: I'm really excited about this. The Jet Propulsion Laboratory group with which I work has already implemented prototype software and protocols needed to make the IPN work. We are working with groups at JPL and NASA to look for useful opportunities to enhance current mission communication plans and begin the process of incrementally building an interplanetary network to support the scientific

exploration of the solar system. There are a number of planned missions to Mars now scheduled between 2001 and 2011, and we hope it may prove possible to have a two-planet network in operation before the end of the decade. We are already certain that we can run conventional or slightly enhanced TCP/IP protocols on board the International Space Station and on board other spacecraft. The deep-space part of the design requires more radical steps, and we are very far along in detailed specifications.

The Internet Chronology

1964
Paul Baran publishes a report named "On Distributed Communications," which outlines the concept of packet switching for computer networks.

1965
The U.S. Advanced Research Project Agency (ARPA) sponsors research into a "cooperative network of time-sharing computers."

1969
The first four nodes of ARPANET are connected at UCLA, Stanford, UCSB, and University of Utah. The first attempt to send a packet crashes the system.

1971
ARPANET expands from four nodes to 15 nodes. Additional sites include MIT, Harvard, and NASA. Ray Tomlinson sends the first e-mail on the ARPANET.

1973
Robert Kahn and Vinton Cerf present the Internet gateway concept in the United Kingdom. Vinton Cerf draws the first gateway diagrams on the back of an envelope.

1975
Satellite links connect computer networks from Hawaii to the continental United States to Great Britain.

1976
Queen Elizabeth sends the first royal e-mail message through the Internet.

1980
ARPANET crashes due to a computer virus.

1984
The Domain Name System (DNS) is created to manage names of Internet computers. Each domain name represents a different type of institution. The original domain names are .edu (education), .gov (government), .mil (military), .com (commercial), .org (organization), and .net (network).

1985
America Online (AOL) is founded. AOL will grow to become the world's largest Internet Service Provider (ISP).

1986
National Science Foundation (NSF) creates high-speed NSFNET to connect super-computing centers at Princeton, Cornell, UCSD, UIUC, and Pittsburgh. The bandwidth of the NSFNET backbone is 56,000 bits per second. The total number of computers on the Internet is about 10,000.

1988
The Computer Emergency Response Team (CERT) is organized to react to security threats. CERT is a response to a worm that affected 10 percent of all Internet computers.

1989
Reseaux IP Europeens (RIPE) is created to provide administration of European networks. The total number of computers on the Internet is more than 100,000.

1990
ARPANET ceases operation.

1991
Tim Berners-Lee develops the World Wide Web (WWW) at CERN, Switzerland. The total number of computers on the Internet exceeds one million. Philip Zimmerman releases Pretty Good Privacy (PGP). PGP allows encrypted data to be sent across the Internet. Connections to the Internet have been added all around the world, including Thailand, Cyprus, and even Antarctica!

The Internet Chronology

MARC ANDREESSEN is known as the creator of the Center for Supercomputing Applications (NCSA). He is also the cocreator of Netscape Communications, Inc., and he led the team which created Netscape Navigator, a World Wide Web browser for MS Windows, Macintosh, and Xwindows platforms.

TIM BERNERS-LEE invented the World Wide Web (WWW), an Internet-based hypermedia initiative for global information sharing. He now works at the Massachusetts Institute of Technology (MIT) as director of the World Wide Web Consortium (W3), which coordinates the Web's development and ensures its stability as the Web continues to grow and to evolve.

PHIL ZIMMERMANN invented the encryption program, Pretty Good Privacy (PGP). PGP became the most widely used e-mail encryption in the world. He currently serves as chief crytogapher at Hush Communications, which delivers security solutions for corporate and personal use.

John Chambers

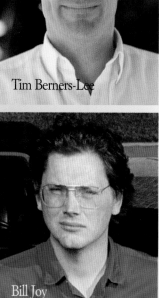

Tim Berners-Lee

Jerry Yang

Bill Joy

David Filo

JOHN CHAMBERS is the president and CEO of Cisco Systems, the worldwide leader in networking for the Internet.

BILL JOY is a cofounder of Sun Microsystems, the source for Java Technology. For his work on the Berkeley UNIX, introducing virtual memory and internetworking, Joy received the ACM Grace Murray Hopper Award.

DAVID FILO & JERRY YANG are the cofounders of Yahoo, one of the first Web directories providing links to thousands of Web sites around the world. Now Yahoo has expanded from merely a Web directory to a Web service center that includes auctions, instant messaging, and other special-interest clubs.

Opposite: an aerial view of the CERN at Geneva.

1992
The Internet Society (ISOC) is formed to develop Internet protocol standards and to promote cooperation for societal issues.

1993
The Web browser Mosaic is introduced. The U.S. White House creates its first Web site. Yahoo!, the Internet portal, begins operation.

1995
NSFNET no longer carries public Internet traffic. Most traffic is now handled by public companies like WorldCom, AT&T, and Sprint. WorldCom and the NSF activate the very high performance Backbone Network Service (BNS). Sun releases the programming language Java. Netscape goes public on the NASDAQ, igniting the Internet stock market boom of the late 1990s.

1998
The Internet Corporation for Assigned Names and Numbers (ICANN) is formed to manage IP addresses and domain names on the Internet.

1999
Internet 2 is expanded to connect Europe to North America. The Internet includes more than 43 million registered IP addresses and nearly 10 million Web servers in 171 countries around the world.

2001
AOL surpasses 30 million users. The Code Red worm provides another security threat on the Internet. ICANN activates two new domain names: .biz and .info. There are 110 million Internet hosts with 28 million Web servers. The Internet continues to grow and to evolve.

Glossary

analog (A-nuhl-og) A way to represent information using changing values like voltages. Telephones use analog signals to send voice sounds.

application (a-pluh-KAY-shuhn) A software program that allows a user to perform a certain task. Examples of applications are word processors, spreadsheets, and games.

ARPANET (Advanced Research Project Agency Network) The original computer network that evolved to become the Internet. It began as a project sponsored by the U.S. Department of Defense ARPA. The original ARPANET consisted of computers at four American universities and began operation in 1969. It was decomissioned in 1990.

backbone (BAK-bohn) A very high speed network that carries large amounts of Internet traffic.

bandwidth (BAND-with) A measurement of how many bits of data can be transmitted each second.

binary (BY-nuh-ree) A numbering system using only the numbers 0 and 1.

bit (BIHT) The smallest unit of data, equal to either a 0 or a 1.

business-to-business (B2B) A use of the Internet for performing business directly between two companies. An example is a car company using the Internet to place orders with a steel company. The Internet can allow companies to complete business transactions quicker, using less money.

coaxial cable (koh-AK-see-uhl KAY-bul) A type of cable with a metal core surrounded by insulation, commonly used for cable and for television connections.

cookie (KUH-kee) A small file used to keep track of an Internet user's activity on Web sites.

digital (DIH-juh-tuhl) A way to represent information using numbers.

DNS (Domain Name Service) A database that matches e-mail, Web, and other addresses to the IP address of a specific computer.

DSL (Digital Subscriber Line) A protocol that allows high-speed data connections on existing copper wires used for telephone lines.

encode (in-KOHD) To place a message into a certain format. A piece of text must be encoded with HTML tags in order to be viewed on the WWW.

encryption (in-KRIP-shun) A method to code and to decode messages using mathematical formulas.

Ethernet (EE-thur-neht) A high-speed protocol to send information between computers over short distances. Slightly different Ethernet types send data at 10 million, 100 million, billion or 10 billion bits per second.

fiber-optic cables (FY-ber OP-tik KAY-bul) Thin strands of glass in casing used to connect computers together at very high speeds.

firewall (FYR-wol) A single computer or system of computers, that protects networks by controlling which packets can enter a network.

gateway (GAYT-way) A special computer that forwards packets from one network into another. Gateways, now called routers, allowed different types of networks to connect.

hacker (HA-ker) A person who uses computer programming or networking knowledge to gain access to computer networks and systems. Some hackers use their knowledge to cause damage to computer files or to steal information. The FBI arrested Kevin Mitnick for illegal hacking in 1995.

hardware (HAHRD-wehr) Physical components of computer systems. This includes computers, modems, monitors, and keyboards.

hermetically-sealed (her-MEHT-ik-lee-SEELD) Something that is closed so tightly or perfectly that it does not allow air or water in or out.

HTML (Hypertext Markup Language) Special codes used to mark text, pictures, and other data so that browsers can display Web pages properly on a computer screen.

HTTP (Hypertext Transfer Protocol) A protocol used to send Web pages between servers and users.

IANA (Internet Assigned Numbers Authority) An organization that assigned Internet domain names and IP addresses. These responsibilities have been handled by ICANN since 1998.

iMODE (EYE-mohd) A mobile Interenet service available in Japan. Users of iMODE can receive email and other Internet services through portable telephones or Personal Data Assistants (PDAs).

infrastructure (IN-fruh-struk-cher) The underlying machines and cables that connecti a computer network.

Internet 2 (IN-ter-net TOO) A group of research institutions developing new technologies and services for the Internet.

IP address (I-PEE UH-drehs) A set of numbers used to identify individual computers on the Internet. An example is 10.4.5.2.

IPN (InterPlaNet) (Interplanetary Internet) Also known as InterPlaNet, the IPN will allow computer communications over extremely long distances in space. NASA's Jet Propulsion Laboratory (JPL) is working on the standards and the technologies for this network that will support future space exploration.

ISDN (Integrated Services Digital Network) A communications protocol that permits high-speed digital Internet connections through copper telephone lines.

ISP (Internet Service Provider) ISPs provide connections for the internet and for businesses.

LAN (Local Area Network) A small, private network in a home or business that connects multiple computers together. Computers connected on a LAN are close together. Ethernet uses technology to create LANs.

microchip (MY-kro-chip) A small, but vital, part of computers that perform functions like adding and copying. Microchips enable computers to become small and cheap enough to be widely available. Intel created the first computer processor using microchips. It was called the 8080.

modem (MOH-duhm) A device that converts digital signals from a computer to analog signals for telephones.

Mosaic (moh-ZAY-ik) The name for an early type of browser software used for viewing HTML files on the Internet.

NAP (Network Access Point) Regional locations where ISPs and backbone carriers connect to each other so data can travel between networks.

network (NEHT-werk) A collection of computers connected together to share information.

NGI (Next Generation Internet) A U.S. government project to build a new, faster Internet.

Glossary

NOC (Network Operations Center) An NOC monitors computer networks to fix problems. Each ISP has one or more NOCs to monitor their portion of the Internet.

ontology (ahn-TAH-luh-jee) A protocol used to connect two computers using different communications lines. PPP can be used to connect ISDN, high-speed serial lines, and normal telephone lines. Most computers use PPP to connect to the Internet with modems.

packet (PA-kit) A specified number of bits arranged in the format used by a particular protocol.

packet-switching (PA-kit SWIH-ching) A method of sending data that separates large pieces of data into smaller packets for efficient delivery to the destination.

PPP (Point to Point Protocol) A protocol used to connect two computers using different types of communications lines. PPP can be used to connect through ISDN, high-speed serial lines, and telephone lines. Most computers use PPP to connect to the Internet with modems.

protocol (PRO-tuh-kol) A set of rules used between computers for a particular purpose. Some examples of network protocols are TCP, IP, and HTTP.

RFC (Request For Comment) A document that publishes specific protocol rules or policies for the Internet.

router (RAU-ter) A computer that connects different networks together and sends packets toward their destination.

Semantic Web A more advanced version of the WWW. On the Semantic Web, information is stored in ways that enable computers, as well as humans, to interpret data and make decisions and connections. This will allow more useful searches for specific information. Computer agents will automatically process information to make useful decisions for humans. An example would be automatically rescheduling an appointment if an airline cancelled a flight.

software (SOFT-wair) A program or set of programs designed to perform specific functions on a computer.

TCP (Transmission Control Protocol) A protocol used to control the sending of information on the Internet. Robert Kahn and Vinton Cerf wrote this protocol in the 1970s. TCP counts, orders, and checks individual packets for errors. It ensures that all parts of a particular message are received and are delivered to an application, like e-mail, for processing.

URL (Uniform Resource Locator) Used to identify computers and files running particular protocols, most commonly on the World Wide Web.

virus (VY-ruhs) A software program designed to cause damage to computer files or other programs.

WAP (Wireless Application Protocol) A protocol that allows wireless devices, like cellular telephones, to connect to the Internet.

Web site (WEB SYT) A single computer or groups of computers that store files, programs, and services that are accessible on computer networks.

worm (WERM) A type of virus program that copies itself from one computer to another.

Additional Resources

For further information about the Internet, check out these books and Web sites.

Books

Haag, Tim and Wendy Chang. *Internet for Kids.* California: Teacher Created Materials, 1996.

Leebow, Ken. *300 Incredible Things for Kids on the Internet.* New York: Mass Market Paperback, 2000.

Moss, Francis, Ted Pedersen, and Valerie Costantino. *Internet for Kids: A Beginner's Guide to Surfing the Net.* New York: Price Stern Sloan Publishing, 1997.

Nelson, Stephen. *Smart Guide to the Internet.* New York: Barnes & Noble Books, 1999.

Web Sites

www.cybergeography.org
www.internet4kids.com
www.internetvalley.com
www.kiddonet.com (Kids Internet Portal)
www.kir.org (Kids Internet Radio)
www.pbskids.org/fun_and_games
www.warnerbros.com/ltti/homepage.html
www.wcom.com/cerfsup
www.w3.org

Index

About the Author

Michael Eck is a Network Engineer at a global financial services firm in New York City, where his responsibilities include network design; high-level network troubleshooting; network operations procedures and policies; and assessment and maintenance of network management systems. Prior to joining Network Operations, Michael worked at Bloomberg L.P. in New York. During his six-year tenure with Bloomberg, Michael served first as a Technical Analyst, managing a team responsible for troubleshooting on Bloomberg's proprietary hardware. Promoted to Network Engineer, he then managed a team of network analysts that helped to deploy and to maintain the world's largest private frame relay network.

Michael graduated magna cum laude from American University, Washington, D.C., with a B.A. in History. Recently published in his company-wide electronic technology newsletter, Michael received high praise for his article on Entuity's Eye of the Storm network-management tool.

Michael enjoys reading, running, cooking, and spending time with his wife and their two cats. A five-time marathoner, Michael is a new convert to the sport of adventure racing. Michael completed the 320-mile Eco-Challenge World Championships in Malaysian Borneo and in New Zealand.

Photo Credits